Build-a-Skill Instant Books

Consonant Blends and Digraphs

Written by
Kim Cernek

Editors: Vicky Shiotsu and Stacey Faulkner
Illustrators: Jenny Campbell and Darcy Tom
Cover Illustrator: Rick Grayson
Designer: The Development Source
Art Director: Moonhee Pak
Project Director: Betsy Morris

Table of Contents

Introduction

About the Build-a-Skill Instant Books Series

The *Build-a-Skill Instant Books* series features a variety of reproducible instant books that focus on important reading and math skills covered in the primary classroom. Each instant book is easy to make, and once children become familiar with the basic formats that appear throughout the series, they will be able to make new books with little help. Children will love the unique, manipulative quality of the books and will want to read them over and over again as they gain mastery of basic learning skills!

About the Build-a-Skill Instant Books: Consonant Blends and Digraphs

This book features common blends and digraphs in fun and easy-to-make instant books. Children will develop fine motor skills and practice following directions as they cut, fold, and staple the reproducible pages together to make strip books, shape books, word wallets, and more! As children read and reread their instant books, they will strengthen their decoding skills and increase their sight word vocabulary.

Refer to the Table of Contents to help with lesson planning. Choose instant book activities that fit with the curriculum goals in your regular or ELL classroom. Use the instant books to practice skills or introduce new ones. Directions for making the instant books appear on pages 3 and 4. These should be copied and sent along with the book patterns when assigning a bookmaking activity as homework.

Making and Using the Instant Books

All of the instant books in this resource require only one or two pieces of paper. Copy the pages on white copy paper or card stock, or use colored paper to jazz up and vary the formats. Children will love personalizing their instant books by coloring them, adding construction paper covers, or decorating them with collage materials such as wiggly eyes, ribbon, and stickers. Customize the instant books by adding extra pages, or by creating your own Flip Book with the reproducible on page 32.

Children can make instant books as an enrichment activity when their regular classwork is done, as a learning center activity during guided reading time, or as a homework assignment. They can place completed instant books in their classroom book boxes and then read and reread the books independently or with a reading buddy. After children have had many opportunities to read their books in school, send the books home for extra skill-building practice. Encourage children to store the books in a special box that they have labeled "I Can Read Box."

Directions for Making the Instant Books

There are seven basic formats for the instant books in this guide. The directions appear below for quick and easy reference. The directions are written *to* the child, in case you would like to send the bookmaking activities home as homework. Just copy the directions and attach them to the instant book pages.

Picture Book, pages 5 and 6

1. Trace the dotted letters.
2. Cut apart the cards on the page.
3. Staple the pages together to make a book.
4. Practice reading your words!

Shape Book, pages 7, 10, 11, 20, 21, 22

1. Write the missing letters on each word card.
2. Cut out the shape and the word cards.
3. Staple the word cards to the shape.
4. Practice reading your words!

Word Wallet, pages 8–9, 13–14, and 18–19

1. Trace the dotted letters on the wallet.
2. Cut out the wallet. Fold it in half along the solid middle line.
3. Staple where shown. Tape the outer edges. Fold the wallet closed.
4. Write the missing letters on the word cards.
5. Cut out the word cards. Sort them into the correct pockets.

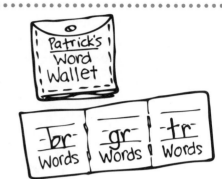

Fold-a-Book, pages 12 and 28

1. Cut along the solid dark lines.
2. Flip the booklet over so that page 4 is on your right.
3. Glue page 5 to the middle of the booklet.
4. Fold page 4 over page 5. Fold over pages 3, 2, and 1.
5. Trace the letters on each page. Draw a picture on page 5.

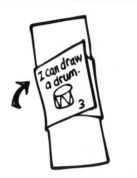

Flip Book, pages 15 and 16

1. Cut out the flip book and letter cards.
2. Staple the cards to the flip book.
3. Finish writing each word.
4. Practice reading your words!

Strip Book, pages 17, 23–24, 25–26, 29, and 30–31

1. Finish the book by writing the missing letters, or words.
2. Cut out the strips.
3. Put the pages in order. Staple them on the left.

Optional: Make and decorate a construction paper cover, and color the pictures.

Chain of Words, page 27

1. Finish the book by writing the missing letters.
2. Color the pictures.
3. Cut out the strips.
4. Glue the strips together to make a paper chain.

Build-a-Skill Instant Books • Consonant Blends and Digraphs © 2015 Creative Teaching Press

My br Picture Book

_____

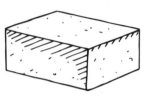

br**ick**

br**anch**

br**ide**

br**aid**

br**ush**

br**oom**

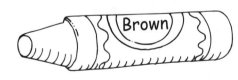

br**own**

_____'s

Great Words!

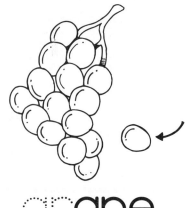

gr ape

gr ass

gr ill

Green

green

gr in

Build-a-Skill Instant Books • Consonant Blends and Digraphs © 2015 Creative Teaching Press

Shape Book

Staple cards here.

My Word Tree

_____

tr uck 	____ack
____ip	____ee
____ash	____ap

Word Wallet

br, gr, tr

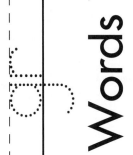

Words

tr

Words

gr

Words

br

Word Wallet

_____'s

Build-a-Skill Instant Books • Consonant Blends and Digraphs © 2015 Creative Teaching Press

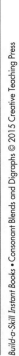

Wallet Words

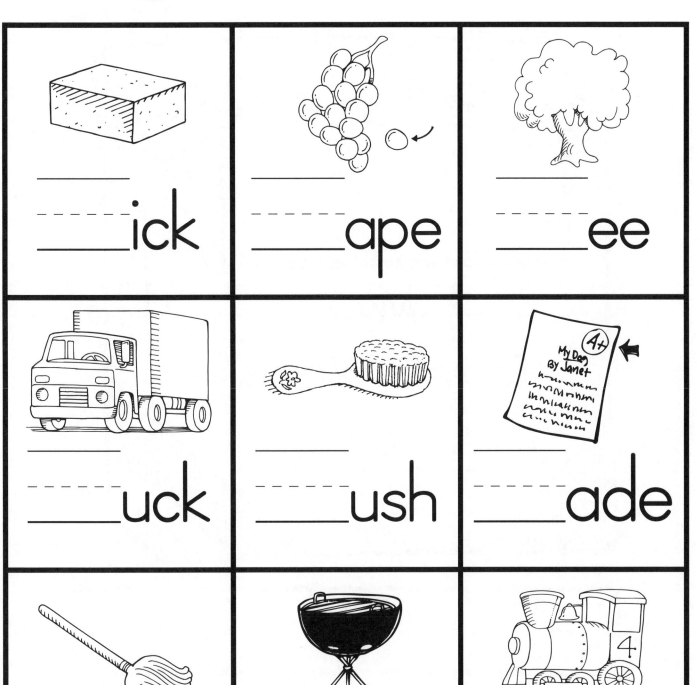

____ick

____ape

____ee

____uck

____ush

____ade

____oom

____ill

____ain

My
Crayon Words

by _____

Staple cards here.

_____ ab 	_____ own
_____ ow	_____ ib
_____ y	_____ ayon

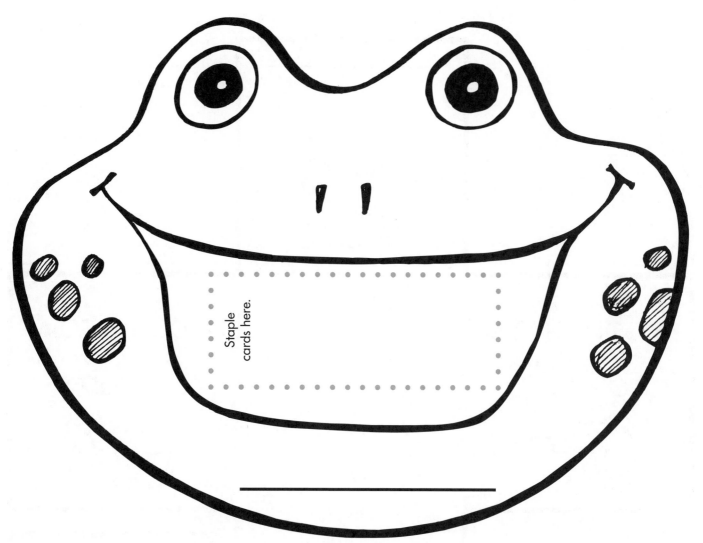

Staple cards here.

_____

Fred Frog's Lunch	_____ame
_____ee	_____uit
_____og	_____ost

Fold-a-Book

I Can Draw! Jack

1 _____

- - - - - - - - -

_____

I Can Draw!

I can draw a drill.

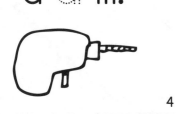

4

I can draw a drum.

3

I can draw a dress.

2

I can draw a dragon.

5

Build-a-Skill Instant Books • Consonant Blends and Digraphs © 2015 Creative Teaching Press

Word Wallet

Words

Words

Words

Word
Wallet

___'s

Words

Words

Words

Tape here.

Staple here.

Staple here.

Tape here.

Fold here.

Tape here.

cr
Words

dr
Words

fr
Words

Wallet Words

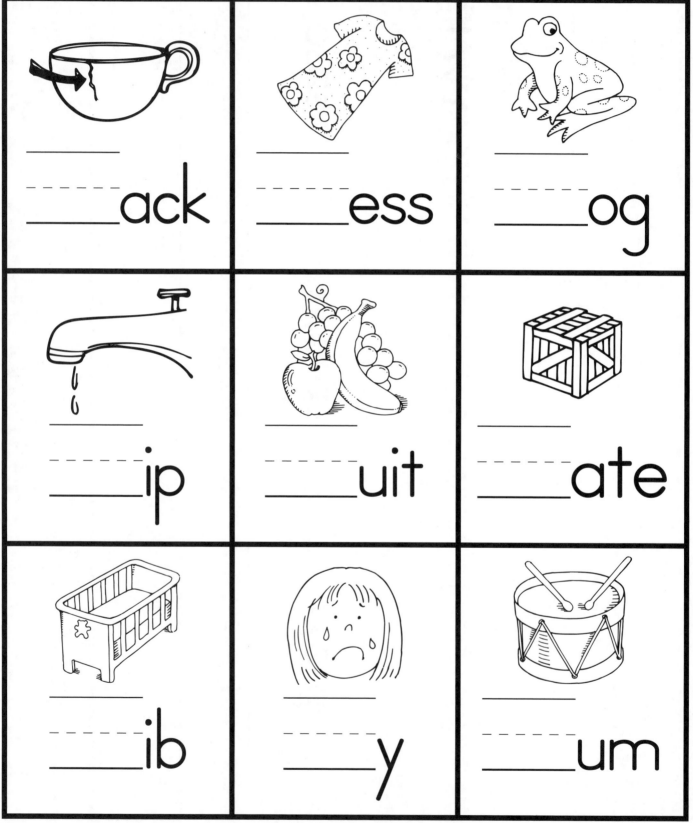

____ack

____ess

____og

____ip

____uit

____ate

____ib

____y

____um

Staple word cards here.

I can read cl ock

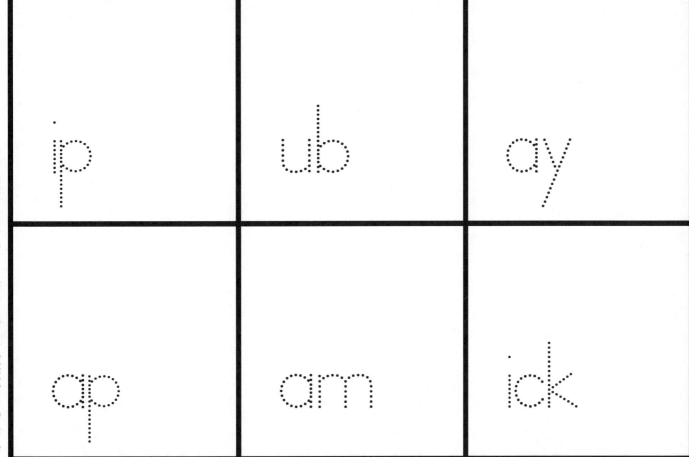

Build-a-Skill Instant Books • Consonant Blends and Digraphs © 2015 Creative Teaching Press

Staple word cards here.

I can read fl ash

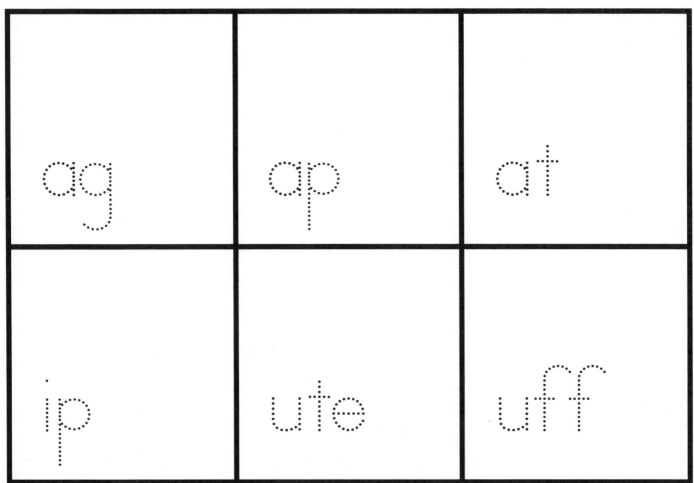

ag   ap   at

ip   ute   uff

_____'s Word Book

1

____
____ate

2

____
____obe

3

____
____ant

4

____
____ad

5

____
____ane

6

Word Wallet

cl, pl, sl

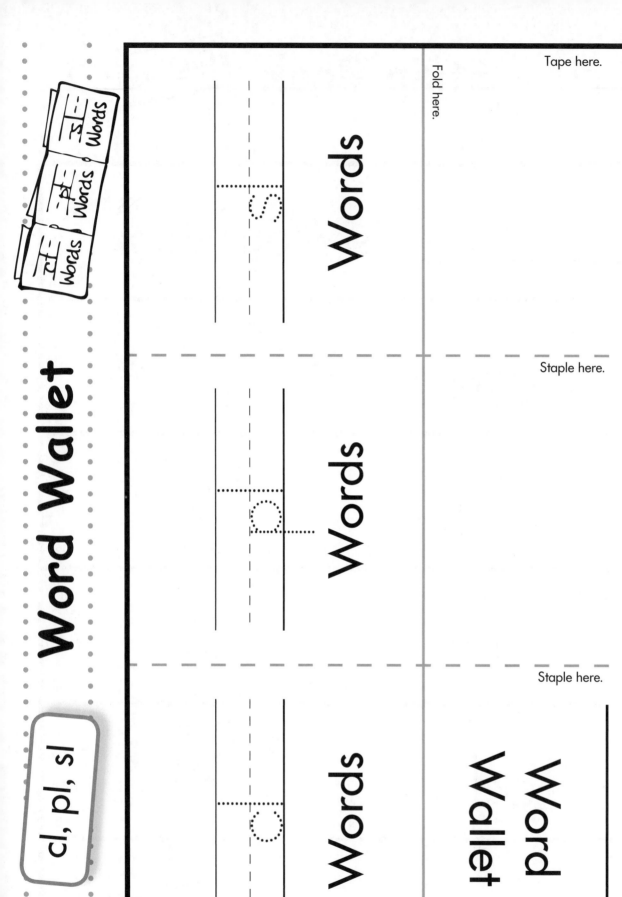

Words

Words

Words

s

p

c

Words
Wallet

's

Tape here.

Fold here.

Staple here.

Staple here.

Tape here.

Wallet Words

_____ ate

_____ ide

_____ ock

_____ ed

_____ ap

_____ ant

_____ own

_____ ug

_____ eep

Build-a-Skill Instant Books • Consonant Blends and Digraphs © 2015 Creative Teaching Press

sk | # Shape Book

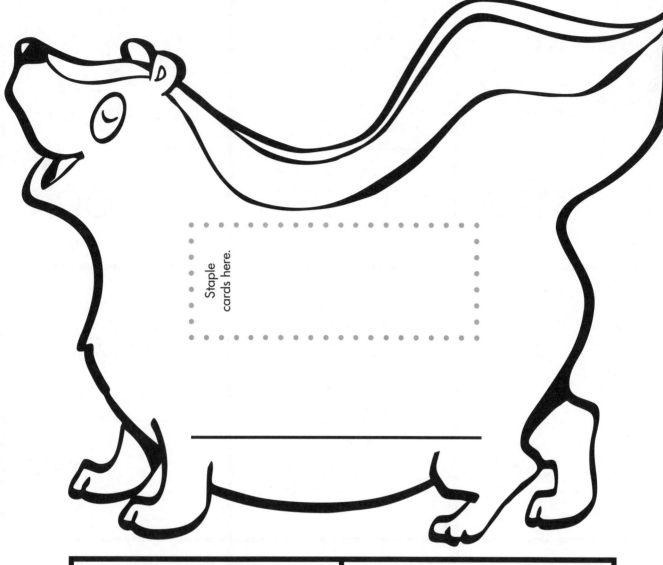

Staple cards here.

_____

Skippy **Sk**unk's Words	_____irt
_____ip	_____in
_____ate	_____unk

Shape Book

Star Words
Tim

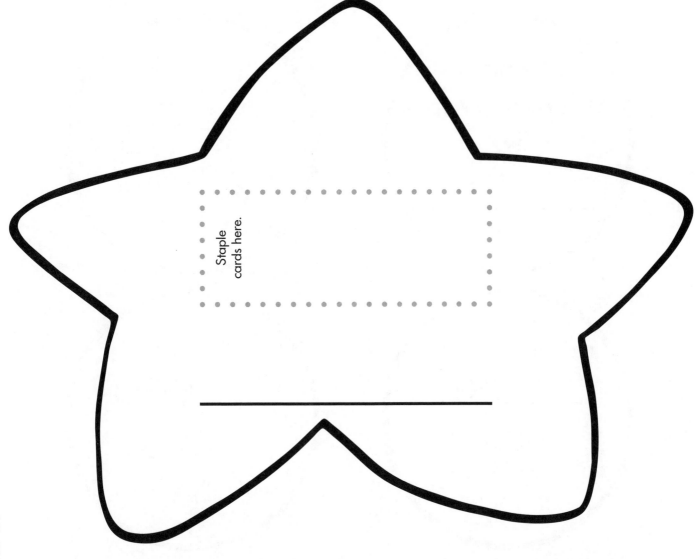

Staple cards here.

_____

Star Words	_____ amp
_____ ill	_____ ick
_____ op STOP	_____ ep

Shape Book

My Book
of Sweet Words
by
Damon

My Book
of **Sw**eet Words
by
_____

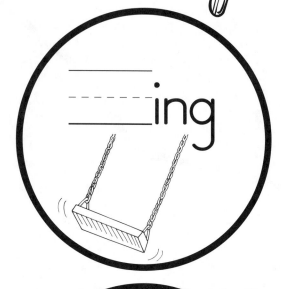

_____ing

_____eet

_____eep

_____im

_____itch

At the Park

by _____

1

I like to

_____

- - - - - - - - - - - -

_____ •

2

I like to

_____

- - - - - - - - - - - -

_____ •

3

I like to _____

4

I like to

_____

5

I like the park!

6

Build-a-Skill Instant Books • Consonant Blends and Digraphs © 2015 Creative Teaching Press

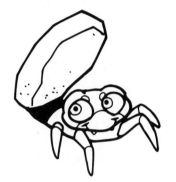

Spot the Spider

_____'s Book

1

Here is a spider.

2

His name is Spot.

He likes to spin.

3

Spot the Spider

Spot has two friends.
Here is Snail.
Here is Snake.

4

Spot, Snail, and
Snake smell a cake.

5

Spot, Snail, and
Snake have big smiles!

6

Build-a-Skill Instant Books • Consonant Blends and Digraphs © 2015 Creative Teaching Press

_____'s **Ch**ain of Words

_____alk

_____ain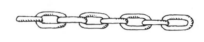

_____eese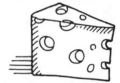

_____air

_____ase

_____eck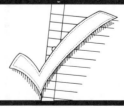

_____ick

Build-a-Skill Instant Books • Consonant Blends and Digraphs © 2015 Creative Teaching Press

1 _____

- - - - - - - - - -

_____

At the
Shore

I see
a shark.

4

I see
a shell.

3

2 I see a ship.

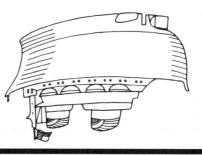

I see the
sun shine!

5

Strip Book

What Is This?
by Terrance ??

What Is This?

by _____

1

What is this?
This is a whale.

2

What is this?
This is thirteen.

13

3

What is this?
This is a wheel.

4

What is this?
This is a thorn.

5

_____ 's

Farm Book

1

There are five

yellow _____.

2

There are four

shy _____.

3

Build-a-Skill Instant Books • Consonant Blends and Digraphs © 2015 Creative Teaching Press

There are _____

pink pigs.

4

There are two

_____ cats.

5

There is one

busy _____.

6

Flip Book

Staple word cards here.

Build-a-Skill Instant Books • Consonant Blends and Digraphs © 2015 Creative Teaching Press